*Dedicated to
my Mother, Mimi, Jayden, Lily, Dr. Kurt Newman
& all the warriors around the world*

Once upon a time, I was a normal kid
who liked to do normal kid things.

I would run and climb, jump and dance,
but my favorite thing to do,
was to play on the swings.

When I turned six, I got really sick.
My mom did not know what to do.

She took me
to the hospital to see what was wrong,
and the doctor said that it was bad news.

He said that I was sicker than sick, but I would feel better if I had surgery.

So, a nurse took me into a big white room, where they gave me medicine so I could fall asleep.

Then the doctor started operating on me.

When I woke up, I felt great. The sickness was gone; the surgery was a success!

As I sat up in the hospital bed,
I looked down at my tummy and
boy, was it a mess!

On my tummy was a scar that was really big! It stretched long and wide.

As I looked at the scar on my tummy, all I could see was ugly, so I sat on my hospital bed and cried.

That's when my mommy said "Please don't cry, you are beautiful inside and out."

"You are a warrior! The toughest of the tough and now everyone can see."

"You went to battle and won the war and now your scar is your body's way of shouting

"Sometimes people won't understand. Some people may even have not so nice words to say."

"Yes, your scar is different and being different is okay. EVERYONE is different in their own special way."

"No matter what happens, remember my words because everything I've said is true."

"Most importantly never forget,
no matter how many scars you have,
I will always love you."

Every day since, I've held my head high and have worn my scar so proud.

Without me saying a word everyone knows that I'm a warrior, because my scar shouts it for me very loud!

About The Author

Jameeliah Joy Hadley is a wife, stay at home mother of 3 kids, and a childhood cancer survivor.

Made in the USA
San Bernardino, CA
03 April 2018